THE MEASURE
OF OUR LIVES

THE MEASURE OF OUR LIVES

A Gathering of Wisdom

—

TONI MORRISON

FOREWORD BY ZADIE SMITH

ALFRED A. KNOPF · NEW YORK · TORONTO · 2019

THIS IS A BORZOI BOOK
PUBLISHED BY ALFRED A. KNOPF AND ALFRED A. KNOPF CANADA

www.aaknopf.com

www.penguinrandomhouse.ca

Knopf, Borzoi Books, and the colophon are registered trademarks
of Penguin Random House LLC.
Knopf Canada and colophon are trademarks of Penguin Random House Canada Limited.

A version of the Foreword first appeared as "Daughters of Toni: A Remembrance" by Zadie Smith
in PEN America as part of "Tribute to Toni Morrison (1931–2019)" on August 7, 2019.

Library of Congress Control Number: 2019952413
ISBN 978-0-525-65929-7 (hardcover) | ISBN 978-0-525-65930-3 (ebook)

Library and Archives Canada Cataloguing in Publication
Title: The measure of our lives : a gathering of wisdom / Toni Morrison ; foreword by Zadie Smith.
Names: Morrison, Toni, author.
Identifiers: Canadiana (print) 20190202149 | Canadiana (ebook) 20190202165 |
ISBN 9780735280236 (hardcover) | ISBN 9780735280243 (HTML)
Subjects: LCSH: Morrison, Toni—Quotations.
Classification: LCC PS3563.08749 M43 2019 | DDC 813/.54—dc23

Jacket photograph by Bernard Gotfryd/Getty Images
Jacket design by John Gall

Manufactured in the United States of America
First Edition

FOREWORD

I READ TONI MORRISON'S EARLY NOVELS very young, probably a little too young, when I was around ten years old. I couldn't always follow her linguistic experiments or the density of her metaphoric expressions, but at that age what mattered more even than her writing was the fact of her. Her books lined our living room shelves and appeared in multiple copies, as if my mother was trying to reassure herself that Morrison was here to stay. It's hard now, in 2019, to recreate or describe the bottom-less need she answered. There was no "black girl magic," in London, in 1985. Indeed, as far as the broader culture was concerned, there was no black girl anything, outside of singing, dancing, and perhaps running. On my mother's shelves there certainly were "black woman writers," and "Toni" was first amongst them, but no such being was ever mentioned in any class I ever attended, and I can't remem-ber ever seeing one on the TV or in the papers or anywhere else. Reading *The Bluest Eye, Sula, Song of Solomon,* and *Tar Baby* for the first time was therefore more than an aesthetic or psychological experience, it was existential. Like a lot of black girls of my generation, I placed Morrison, in her single person, in an impossible role. I wanted to see her name on the spine of a book and feel some of the same lazy assumption and smug confidence of familial relation, of inherited potential, that any Anglo-Saxon boy in school felt—no matter how unlettered or indifferent to literature—whenever he heard the name of William Shakespeare, say, or John Keats. No writer should have to bear such a burden. What's extraordinary about Morrison is that she not only wanted that burden, she was equal to it. She knew we needed her to be not just a writer but a discourse and she became one, making her language out of whole cloth, and conceiving of each novel as a project, as a mission—never as mere entertainment. Just as there is a Keatsian sentence and a Shakespearean one, so Morrison made a sentence distinctly hers, abundant in compulsive, self-generating metaphor, as full of sub-clauses as a piece of 19th century presidential oratory, and always faithful to the central belief that narrative language—inconclusive, non-definitive, ambivalent, twisting, metaphorical narrative language, with its roots in oral culture—can offer a form of wisdom distinct from and in opposition to, as she put it, the "calcified language of the academy or the commodity-driven language of science."

The thwarting of human potential was her great theme, but there was nothing subconscious or accidental about it—she couldn't afford there to be. In *The Bluest Eye,* for example, how do you write about self-loathing without submitting to the same? Or demonizing the habit? Or handing the power of victory precisely to the culture that has created the feeling? All of it had to be thought through, and she thought about all of it, as a working novelist but also as a critic and academic. To me the most astonishing section of her final book of essays, *The Source of Self-Regard,* is the level of sustained academic critique she was able to bring to bear upon her own novels, like an architect walking you through a building she'd made, with the same consciousness of its beauty but also of its use. Toni Morrison put herself in the service of her people, as few writers have ever been called upon to do, and she claimed it as a privilege. A large part of the project was the ennobling of black culture itself and its deliberate encasement in a vocabulary worthy of its glories. To those who considered the entrance to her buildings narrow she had many famous rejoinders. And now—in no small part because of her determination not to be swayed from her project—we of course understand that there are no such things as narrow entrances into the houses of history, experience, and culture. For when it comes to ways of telling, ways of seeing, every man's story is infinite. Every black woman's, too. This infinite terrain is what she opened up for girls like me who had feared otherwise.

Zadie Smith, August 7, 2019

PUBLISHER'S NOTE

Through bricolage—construction or creation from a diverse range of available things—this brief book aims to limn the totality of Toni Morrison's literary vision and achievement. It dramatizes the life of her mind by juxtaposing quotations, one to a page, drawn from her entire body of work, both fiction and nonfiction—from *The Bluest Eye* to *God Help the Child,* from *Playing in the Dark* to *The Source of Self-Regard.*

Its sequence of flashes of revelation—remarkable for their linguistic felicity, keenness of psychological observation, and philosophical profundity—addresses issues of abiding interest in Morrison's work: the reach of language for the ineffable; transcendence through imagination; the self and its discontents; the vicissitudes of love; the whirligig of memory; the singular power of women; the original American sin of slavery; the bankruptcy of racial oppression; the humanity and art of black people.

THE MEASURE
OF OUR LIVES

"We die.

That may be the meaning of life.

But we *do* language.

That may be the measure of our lives."

"My nature is a quiet one, anyway.

As a child I was considered respectful;

as a young woman I was called discreet.

Later on I was thought to have

the wisdom maturity brings."

"Don't you remember being young,
when language was magic without meaning?
When what you could say could not mean?
When the invisible was what imagination
strove to see? When questions and demands
for answers burned so brightly you
trembled with fury at not knowing?"

"Long ago she had given up trying

to be deft or profound or anything

in the company of people

she was not interested in,

who didn't thrill her."

✑

"Sweet, crazy conversations

full of half sentences, daydreams and

misunderstandings more thrilling

than understanding could ever be."

"Their conversation is like

a gently wicked dance: sound meets sound,

curtsies, shimmies, and retires.

Another sound enters but is upstaged

by still another: the two circle each other

and stop. Sometimes their words move

in lofty spirals; other times they take

strident leaps, and all of it is punctuated

with warm-pulsed laughter—like the throb

of a heart made of jelly."

✑

"We substituted

good grammar for intellect;

we switched habits to simulate maturity;

we rearranged lies and called it truth,

seeing in the new pattern of an old idea

the Revelation and the Word."

"In a way, her strangeness, her naïveté,

her craving for the other half of her equation

was the consequence of an idle imagination.

Had she paints, or clay, or knew the discipline

of the dance, or strings; had she anything

to engage her tremendous curiosity and her gift

for metaphor, she might have exchanged the

restlessness and preoccupation with whim for an

activity that provided her with all she yearned for.

And like any artist with no art form,

she became dangerous."

"They ran in the sunlight, creating their own breeze,

which pressed their dresses into their damp skin.

Reaching a kind of square of four leaf-locked trees

which promised cooling,

they flung themselves into the four-cornered shade

to taste their lip sweat and contemplate the wildness

that had come upon them so suddenly."

"I have only to break into the tightness

of a strawberry, and I see summer—its dust

and lowering skies."

✦

"The visionary language

of the doomed reaches

heights of linguistic ardor

with which language of

the blessed and saved

cannot compete."

"Language, when finally it comes,

has the vigor of a felon pardoned after

twenty-one years on hold.

Sudden, raw,

stripped to its underwear."

✍

"Language can never 'pin down'

slavery, genocide, war.

Nor should it yearn

for the arrogance to be able to do so.

Its force, its felicity is in its reach

toward the ineffable."

"In this here place, we flesh;

flesh that weeps, laughs; flesh that dances

on bare feet in grass. Love it. Love it hard.

Yonder they do not love your flesh.

They despise it."

"He couldn't stay there

surrounded by a passel of slaves

whose silence made him imagine

an avalanche seen from a great distance.

No sound, just the knowledge

of a roar he could not hear."

"I welcomed the circling sharks

but they avoided me as if knowing

I preferred their teeth to the chains around my neck

my waist my ankles."

✍

"You accepted like a beast of burden the whip

of a stranger's curse and the mindless menace

it holds along with the scar it leaves as a definition

you spend your life refuting although

that hateful word is only a slim line drawn

on a shore and quickly dissolved in a seaworld

any moment when an equally mindless wave

fondles it like the accidental touch of a finger

on a clarinet stop that the musician

converts into silence in order

to let the true note ring out loud."

❦

"Definitions belonged to the definers,

not the defined."

"If writing is thinking and discovery

and selection and order and meaning,

it is also awe and reverence

and mystery and magic."

"Sunk in the grass of an empty lot

on a spring Saturday, I split the stems

of milkweed and thought about ants

and peach pits and death and

where the world went

when I closed my eyes."

✑

"At some point in life the world's beauty

becomes enough.

You don't need to photograph, paint

or even remember it. It is enough.

No record of it needs to be kept

and you don't need someone

to share it with or tell it to."

✑

"Her mind traveled crooked streets

and aimless goat paths, arriving sometimes

at profundity, other times

at the revelations of a three-year-old.

Throughout this fresh, if common,

pursuit of knowledge, one conviction crowned her

efforts: . . . she knew

there was nothing to fear."

"The City is what they want it to be:

thriftless, warm, scary

and full of amiable strangers.

No wonder they forget pebbly creeks

and when they do not forget

the sky completely

think of it as a tiny piece of information

about the time of day or night."

◈

"There, in the process of writing,

was the illusion, the deception of control,

of nestling up ever closer to meaning."

"Hospitality is gold in this City;

you have to be clever to figure out

how to be welcoming and defensive at the same time.

When to love something and when to quit.

If you don't know how, you can end up out of control

or controlled by some outside thing

like that hard case last winter."

〰

"It is sheer good fortune to miss somebody

long before they leave you."

"All water has a perfect memory

and is forever trying to get back

to where it was. Writers are like that:

remembering where we were,

what valley we ran through,

what the banks were like,

the light that was there and the route back

to our original place."

❦

"All narrative begins for me as listening.

When I read, I listen. When I write,

I listen—for silence, inflection, rhythm, rest."

"The words dance in my head

to the music in my mouth."

—⊛⊛⊛—

"There is a loneliness that can be rocked.

Arms crossed, knees drawn up; holding,

holding on, this motion, unlike a ship's,

smooths and contains the rocker.

It's an inside kind—wrapped tight like skin.

Then there is a loneliness that roams.

No rocking can hold it down. It is alive,

on its own. A dry and spreading thing

that makes the sound of one's own feet going

seem to come from a far-off place."

∽

"There, in the center of that silence

was not eternity but the death of time

and a loneliness so profound

the word itself had no meaning."

~

"Nowadays silence is looked on as odd

and most of my race has forgotten

the beauty of meaning much by saying little.

Now tongues work all by themselves

with no help from the mind."

"She learned the intricacy

of loneliness: the horror of color,

the roar of soundlessness

and the menace

of familiar objects lying still."

ↆↄ

"Lonely, ain't it?"

"Yes, but my lonely is *mine*. Now your lonely is somebody else's. Made by somebody else and handed to you. Ain't that something? A secondhand lonely."

"Lonely was much better than alone."

"The sun and the moon shared the horizon

in a distant friendship,

each unfazed by the other."

"Narrative fiction provides

a controlled wilderness, an opportunity

to be and to become the Other.

The stranger. With sympathy, clarity,

and the risk of self-examination.

In this iteration, for me the author,

Beloved the girl, the haunter, is the ultimate Other.

Clamoring, forever clamoring for a kiss."

ɔɔ

"The danger of sympathizing

with the stranger is the possibility

of becoming a stranger.

To lose one's racial-ized rank

is to lose one's own valued and enshrined

difference."

♕

"What I remember is a picture floating

around out there outside my head.

I mean, even if I don't think it,

even if I die, the picture of what I did,

or knew, or saw is still out there.

Right in the place where it happened."

"As writers,

what we do is remember.

And to remember this world

is to create it."

"A child. New life.

Immune to evil or illness,

protected from kidnap, beatings, rape, racism, insult,

hurt, self-loathing,

abandonment. Error-free.

All goodness. Minus wrath.

So they believe."

"What you do to children matters.

And they might never forget."

"124 was spiteful.

Full of a baby's venom.

The women in the house knew it

and so did the children."

✎

"The presence of evil

was something to be first recognized,

then dealt with, survived, outwitted,

triumphed over."

ℒ

"Whose house is this?

Whose night keeps out the light

In here?

Say, who owns this house?

It's not mine.

I dreamed another, sweeter, brighter

With a view of lakes crossed in painted boats;

Of fields wide as arms open for me.

This house is strange.

Its shadows lie.

Say, tell me, why does its lock fit my key?"

"Misery don't call ahead.

That's why you have to stay awake—

otherwise it just walks on in your door."

"I can be miserable if I want to.

You don't need to try and make it go away.

It shouldn't go away. It's just as sad

as it ought to be and I'm not going

to hide from what's true just because it hurts."

"Now they will rest before shouldering

the endless work they were created to do

down here in Paradise."

"Every now and then she looked around

for tangible evidence

of his having ever been there.

Where were the butterflies? the blueberries?

the whistling reed? She could find nothing,

for he had left nothing

but his stunning absence."

"But to find out the truth

about how dreams die,

one should never take the word

of the dreamer."

◈

"Guileless and without vanity,

we were still in love with ourselves then.

We felt comfortable in our skins,

enjoyed the news that our senses

released to us, admired our dirt,

cultivated our scars, and could not

comprehend this unworthiness."

"Do they still call it infatuation?

That magic ax that chops away the world in one

blow, leaving only the couple standing there

trembling? Whatever they call it,

it leaps over anything, takes the biggest chair,

the largest slice, rules the ground wherever it walks,

from a mansion to a swamp,

and its selfishness is its beauty."

"This is the it you've been looking for."

"What's the world for

if you can't make it up the way you want it?"

"In Ohio seasons are theatrical.

Each one enters like a prima donna,

convinced its performance

is the reason the world has people in it."

"Quiet as it's kept,

there were no marigolds in the fall of 1941.

We thought, at the time, that it was because

Pecola was having her father's baby

that the marigolds did not grow."

"Except for World War II,

nothing ever interfered with the celebration

of National Suicide Day. It had taken place

every January third since 1920,

although Shadrack, its founder,

was for many years the only celebrant."

"They shoot the white girl first.

With the rest they can take their time.

No need to hurry out here."

"The North Carolina Mutual

Life Insurance agent promised

to fly from Mercy to the other side

of Lake Superior at three o'clock.

Two days before the event was to take place

he tacked a note on the door

of his little yellow house."

"Sth, I know that woman.

She used to live with a flock of birds

on Lenox Avenue. Know her husband, too.

He fell for an eighteen-year-old girl

with one of those deepdown, spooky loves

that made him so sad and happy he shot her

just to keep the feeling going."

"Nothing could be taken for granted. Women who loved you tried to cut your throat, while women who didn't even know your name scrubbed your back. Witches could sound like Katharine Hepburn and your best friend could try to strangle you. Smack in the middle of an orchid there might be a blob of jello and inside a Mickey Mouse doll, a fixed and radiant star."

"Along with the idea of romantic love, she was introduced to another—physical beauty. Probably the most destructive ideas in the history of human thought. Both originated in envy, thrived in insecurity, and ended in disillusion."

"Her color is a cross she will always carry."

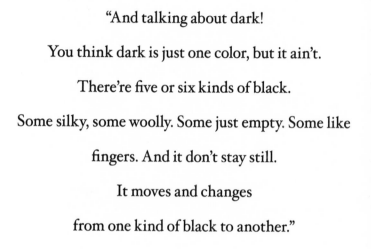

"And talking about dark!

You think dark is just one color, but it ain't.

There're five or six kinds of black.

Some silky, some woolly. Some just empty. Some like

fingers. And it don't stay still.

It moves and changes

from one kind of black to another."

“Now he knew why he loved her so.
Without ever leaving the ground,
she could fly. ‘There must be another one
like you,’ he whispered to her.
‘There’s got to be at least
one more woman like you.’”

೭

"When fear rules,

obedience is the only survival choice."

"More awful than the fear of danger was the fear of looking foolish—of being excited when others were laid back—of being somehow manipulated."

"You looking good."

"Devil's confusion.

He lets me look good long as I feel bad."

"You are nothing but wilderness.

No constraint. No mind."

"The loss pressed down on her chest

and came up into her throat. . . . It was a fine cry—

loud and long—but it had no bottom

and it had no top,

just circles and circles of sorrow."

———⟨∞⟩———

"The women's legs are spread wide open,

so I hum. Men grow irritable,

but they know it's all for them. They relax.

Standing by, unable to do anything but watch,

is a trial, but I don't say a word."

~❧

"You looked at me then

like you knew me, and I thought

it really was Eden, and I couldn't take your

eyes in because I was loving

the hoof marks on your cheeks."

⁓

"She was the third beer.

Not the first one, which the throat receives

with almost tearful gratitude;

nor the second, that confirms and extends

the pleasure of the first. But the third,

the one you drink because it's there,

because it can't hurt, and because

what difference does it make?"

※

"In fact her maturity and blood kinship converted

her passion to fever, so it was more affliction

than affection. It literally knocked her down

at night, and raised her up in the morning,

for when she dragged herself off to bed, having

spent another day without his presence, her heart

beat like a gloved fist against her ribs."

———⊗⊗⊗———

"Where do you get the *right*

to decide our lives? . . . I'll tell you where.

From that hog's gut that hangs

down between your legs. Well, let me tell you

something . . . you will need more than that.

I don't know where you will get it or who will

give it to you, but mark my words,

you will need more than that."

"Fondling their weapons,

feeling suddenly so young and good

they are reminded that guns

are more than decoration, intimidation or comfort.

They are meant."

—❧—

"They rose up like men. We saw them.

Like men they stood."

"A son ain't what a woman say.

A son is what a man do."

"What a man leaves behind is what a man is."

꒰

"Our past is bleak. Our future dim.

But I am not reasonable. A reasonable man

adjusts to his environment.

And unreasonable man does not.

All progress, therefore, depends on the

unreasonable man. I prefer not to adjust

to my environment. I refuse the prison of 'I'

and choose the open spaces of 'we.' "

"Being good to somebody

is just like being mean to somebody. Risky.

You don't get nothing for it."

"Don't be afraid. My telling can't hurt you

in spite of what I have done and

I promise to lie quietly in the dark—weeping

perhaps or occasionally seeing the blood

once more—but I will never again

unfold my limbs to rise up and bare teeth."

"Hate does that.

Burns off everything but itself,

so whatever your grievance is,

your face looks just like your enemy's."

"Anger is better.

There is a sense of being in anger.

A reality and presence. An awareness of worth.

It is a lovely surging."

"He suspected most of the real answers concerning slavery, lynching, forced labor, sharecropping, racism, Reconstruction, Jim Crow, prison labor, migration, civil rights and black revolution movements were all about money. Money withheld, money stolen, money as power, as war. Where was the lecture on how slavery alone catapulted the whole country from agriculture into the industrial age in two decades?
White folks' hatred, their violence, was the gasoline that kept the profit motors running."

※

"I am nothing to you.

You say I am wilderness. I am.

Is that a tremble on your mouth, in your eye?

Are you afraid? You should be."

❧

"My face absent in blue water

you find only to crush it?"

"Perhaps that's what all human relationships

boiled down to: Would you save my life?

or would you take it?"

⚜

"She was fierce in the presence of death,

heroic even, as she was at no other time.

Its threat gave her direction, clarity, audacity."

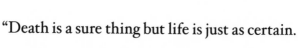

"Death is a sure thing but life is just as certain.

Problem is you can't know in advance."

" 'You in trouble,' she says, yawning.

'Deep, deep trouble. Can't rival the dead for love.

Lose every time.' "

"It had been the longest time

since she had had a rib-scraping laugh.

She had forgotten how deep and down it could be.

So different from the miscellaneous giggles

and smiles she had learned to be content with

these past few years."

"Every sentence, every word,

was new to them and they listened

to what he said like bright-eyed ravens,

trembling in their eagerness

to catch and interpret every sound

in the universe."

"You shout the word—

mind, mind, mind—

over and over and then you laugh,

saying as I live and breathe,

a slave by choice."

"Like friendship, hatred needed more

than physical intimacy; it wanted creativity

and hard work to sustain itself."

❦

"They will blow it, she thought.

Each will cling to a sad little story

of hurt and sorrow—some long-ago trouble and pain

life dumped on their pure and innocent selves.

And each one will rewrite that story forever,

knowing the plot, guessing the theme,

inventing its meaning and dismissing its origin."

"I don't want to be free of you because

I am alive only with you."

"To be given dominion over another

is a hard thing; to wrest dominion over

another is a wrong thing;

to give dominion of yourself to another

is a wicked thing."

$\backsim$

"Say make me, remake me.

You are free to do it and

I am free to let you because look, look.

Look where your hands are. Now."

❧

"She didn't say so,

but it suddenly occurred to her

that good sex was not knowledge.

It was barely information."

"There is no protection.

To be female in this place

is to be an open wound that cannot heal.

Even if scars form,

the festering is ever below."

"You can't own a human being.

You can't lose what you don't own.

Suppose you did own him.

Could you really love somebody

who was absolutely nobody without you?

You really want somebody like that?"

"She told them that the only grace

they could have was the grace they could imagine.

That if they could not see it,

they would not have it."

"It takes a certain intelligence to love like that—

softly, without props. But the world

is such a showpiece, maybe that's why folks

try to outdo it, put everything they feel onstage

just to prove they can think up things too:

handsome scary things like fights to the death,

adultery, setting sheets afire. They fail, of course.

The world outdoes them every time."

"Love is never any better than the lover.

Wicked people love wickedly,

violent people love violently,

weak people love weakly,

stupid people love stupidly,

but the love of a free man is never safe.

There is no gift for the beloved.

The lover alone possesses his gift of love.

The loved one is shorn, neutralized,

frozen in the glare of the lover's inward eye."

"'Gimme hate, Lord,' he whimpered.

'I'll take hate any day. But don't give me love.

I can't take no more love, Lord. I can't carry it. . . .

It's too heavy. Jesus, *you* know, you know all about it.

Ain't it heavy? Jesus? Ain't love heavy?'"

⌭

"We mistook violence for passion,

indolence for leisure,

and thought recklessness was freedom."

"Love is divine only and difficult always. If you think it is easy you are a fool. If you think it is natural you are blind. It is a learned application without reason or motive except that it is God.

You do not deserve love regardless of the suffering you have endured. You do not deserve love because somebody did you wrong. You do not deserve love just because you want it. You can only earn—by practice and careful contemplation—the right to express it and you have to learn how to accept it. Which is to say you have to earn God. You have to practice God. You have to think God—carefully."

"More than fear of loving bears

or birds bigger than cows,

I fear pathless night. How, I wonder,

can I find you in the dark?"

"Me and you,

we got more yesterday than anybody.

We need some kind of tomorrow."

⬦

"A dead hydrangea is as intricate and lovely

as one in bloom. Bleak sky is as seductive

as sunshine, miniature orange trees

without blossom or fruit

are not defective; they are that."

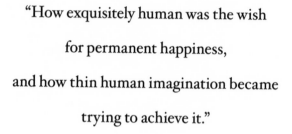

"How exquisitely human was the wish

for permanent happiness,

and how thin human imagination became

trying to achieve it."

"Pain. I seem to have an affection,

a kind of sweettooth for it.

Bolts of lightning, little rivulets of thunder.

And I the eye of the storm."

———— ∞∞∞ ————

"The freezing in hell that comes

before the everlasting fire

where sinners bubble and singe forever."

"Don't ever think I fell for you,

or fell over you. I didn't fall in love,

I rose in it."

❧

"Her passions were narrow but deep."

"Look to yourself. You free.

Nothing and nobody is obliged

to save you but you."

✍

"Freeing yourself was one thing; claiming ownership

of that freed self was another."

"I dream a dream that dreams back at me."

"When she awoke there was a melody in her head

she could not identify or recall ever hearing before.

'Perhaps I made it up,' she thought.

Then it came to her—the name of the song

and all its lyrics just as she had heard it

many times before.

She sat on the edge of the bed thinking,

'There aren't any more new songs

and I have sung all the ones there are.

I have sung them all.

I have sung all the songs there are.'"

"If you surrendered to the air,

you could *ride* it."

∿

"How come it can't fly

no better than a chicken?" . . .

"Too much tail.

All that jewelry weighs it down. Like vanity.

Wanna fly, you got to

give up the shit that weighs you down."

"You your best thing, Sethe. You are."

ATTRIBUTIONS

A NOTE ABOUT THE AUTHOR

Toni Morrison—who died in 2019—wrote eleven novels, from *The Bluest Eye* (1970) to *God Help the Child* (2015). She received the National Book Critics Circle Award and the Pulitzer Prize. In 1993 she was awarded the Nobel Prize in Literature.

A NOTE ON THE TYPE

This book was set in Hoefler Text, designed by Jonathan Hoefler, who was born in 1970. First designed in 1991, Hoefler Text looks to the old-style fonts of the seventeenth century, but it employs a precision and sophistication available only to the late twentieth century.

Composed by North Market Street Graphics,
Lancaster, Pennsylvania
Printed and bound by LSC Communications,
Crawfordsville, Indiana
Designed by Maggie Hinders